WRITTEN AND ILLUSTRATED BY BEV ARMSTRONG

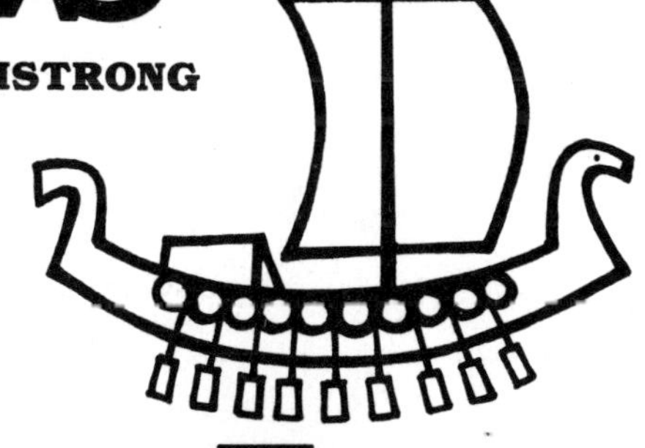

The Learning Works

Designed and edited by
Sherri M. Butterfield

Library of Congress Catalog Number:
92-074099
ISBN 0-88160-220-5
LW 304

Printed in the United States of America.

Current Printing (last digit):
10 9 8 7 6 5 4 3 2 1

Introduction

SUPERDOODLES are books that provide simple, step-by-step instructions for super line drawings. The vehicles in this book may be sketched large for murals or posters, or small for bookmarks and flip books. They may be used individually in separate pictures or combined to illustrate methods of transportation.

As you follow the steps, draw in pencil. Dotted lines appear in some steps. Make these lines light so that they can be easily erased later. When you have finished your drawing, erase all unnecessary lines. To give your drawing a finished look, go over the remaining lines with a colored pencil, crayon, or felt-tipped pen.

If you have trouble drawing wheels or other round objects, consider using a circle template. These handy plastic devices are available at art and office supply stores. The round holes they contain will enable you to create perfect circles in many sizes.

If you enjoy this book, look for other **Learning Works SUPERDOODLES.** Titles in this series include ***Dinosaurs, Mammals, Rain Forest,*** and ***Sports.***

biplane

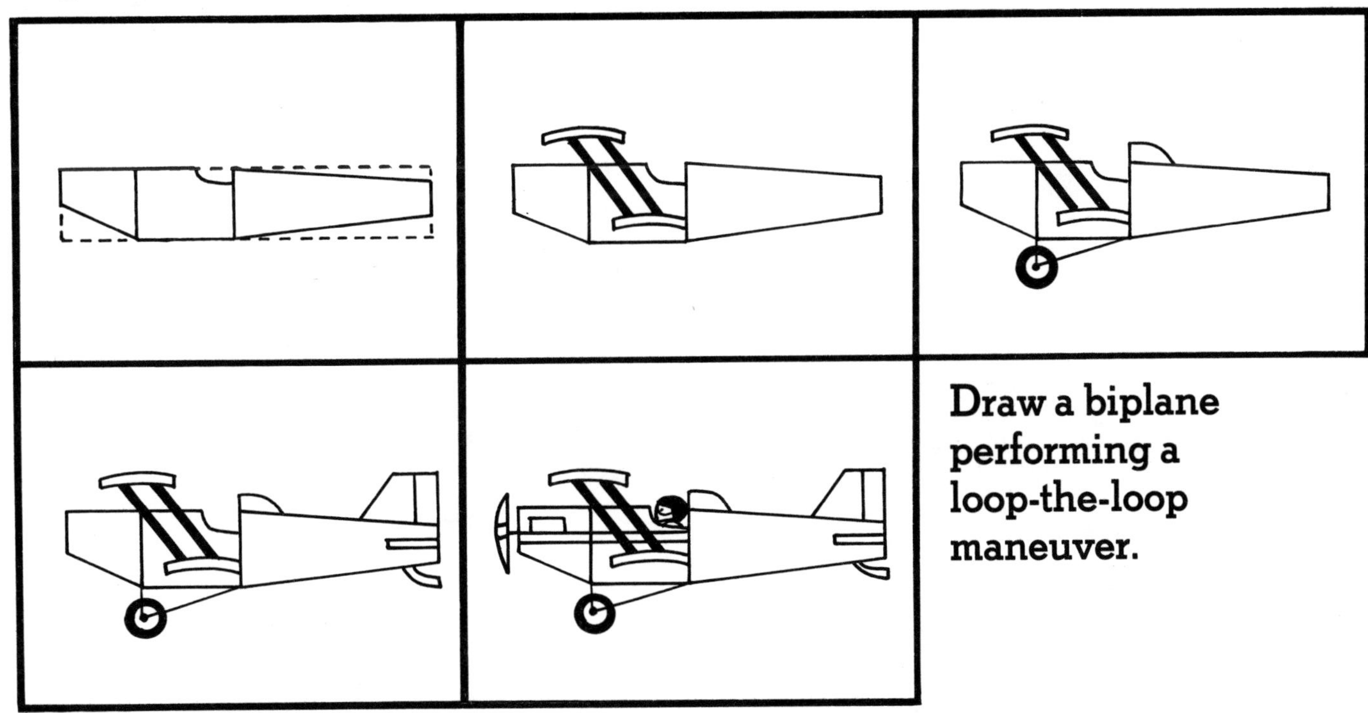

Draw a biplane performing a loop-the-loop maneuver.

bulldozer

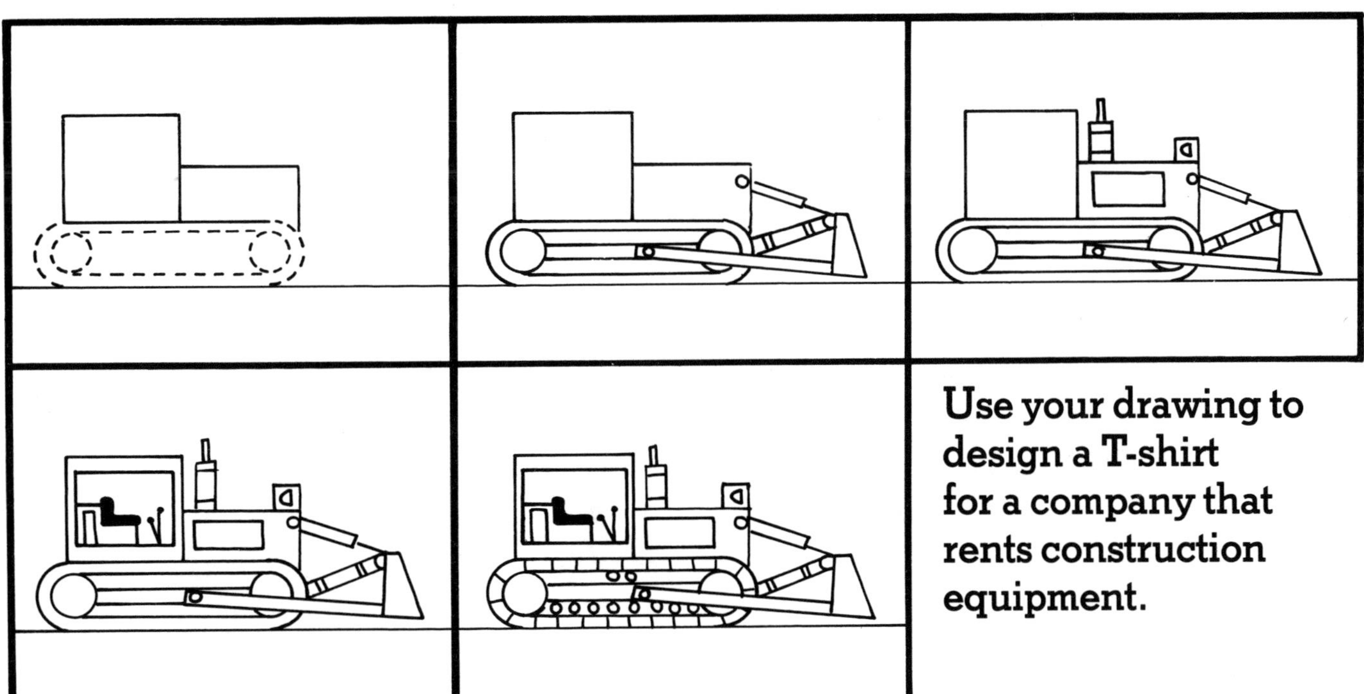

Use your drawing to design a T-shirt for a company that rents construction equipment.

chopper

On a long piece of paper, draw a **BIG** picture of this super chopper. Color it with wild, bright colors.

crane

This truck-mounted crane can turn in all directions. Give it a load of logs to lift.

dragster

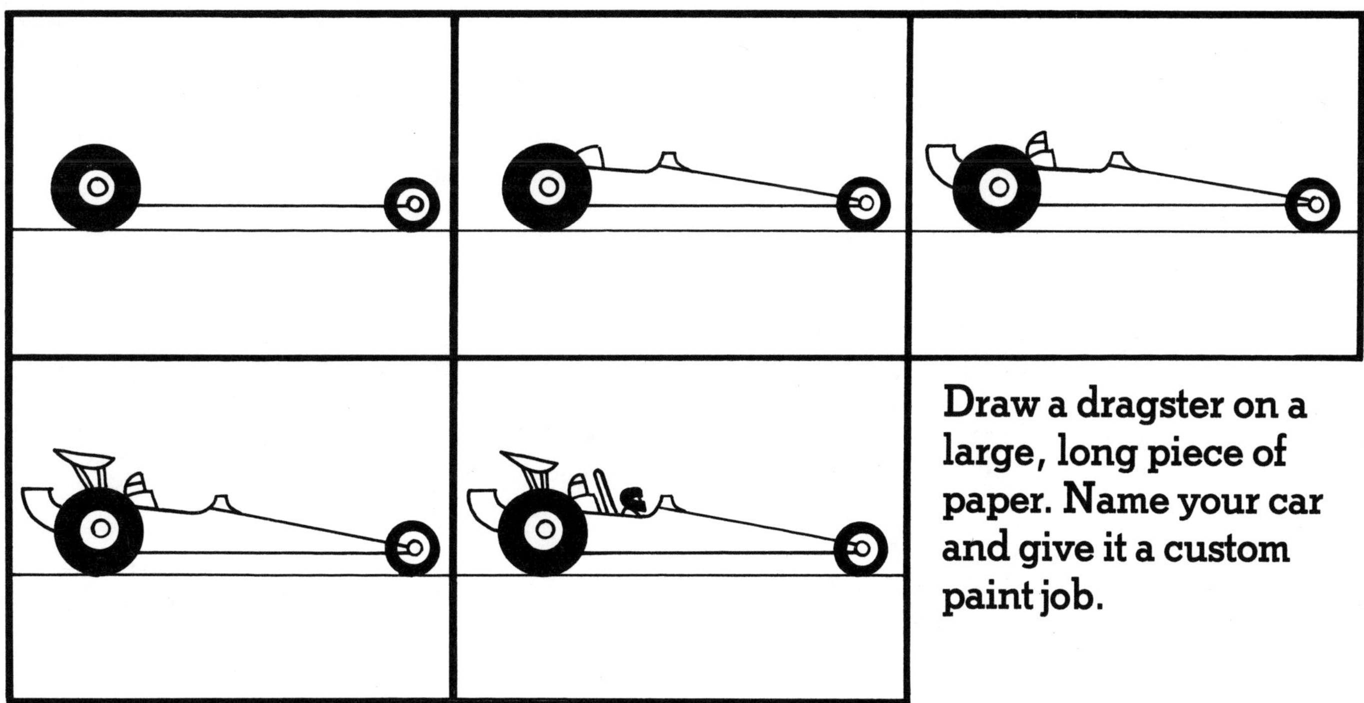

Draw a dragster on a large, long piece of paper. Name your car and give it a custom paint job.

dump truck

This heavy-duty truck can carry a huge load. Fill it with sand or boulders.

dune buggy

Draw yourself in a dune buggy, popping over the top of a dune or racing down a steep slope.

electric car

These tiny cars are useful for short errands. Draw an electric car that is being used to deliver pizza.

fire truck

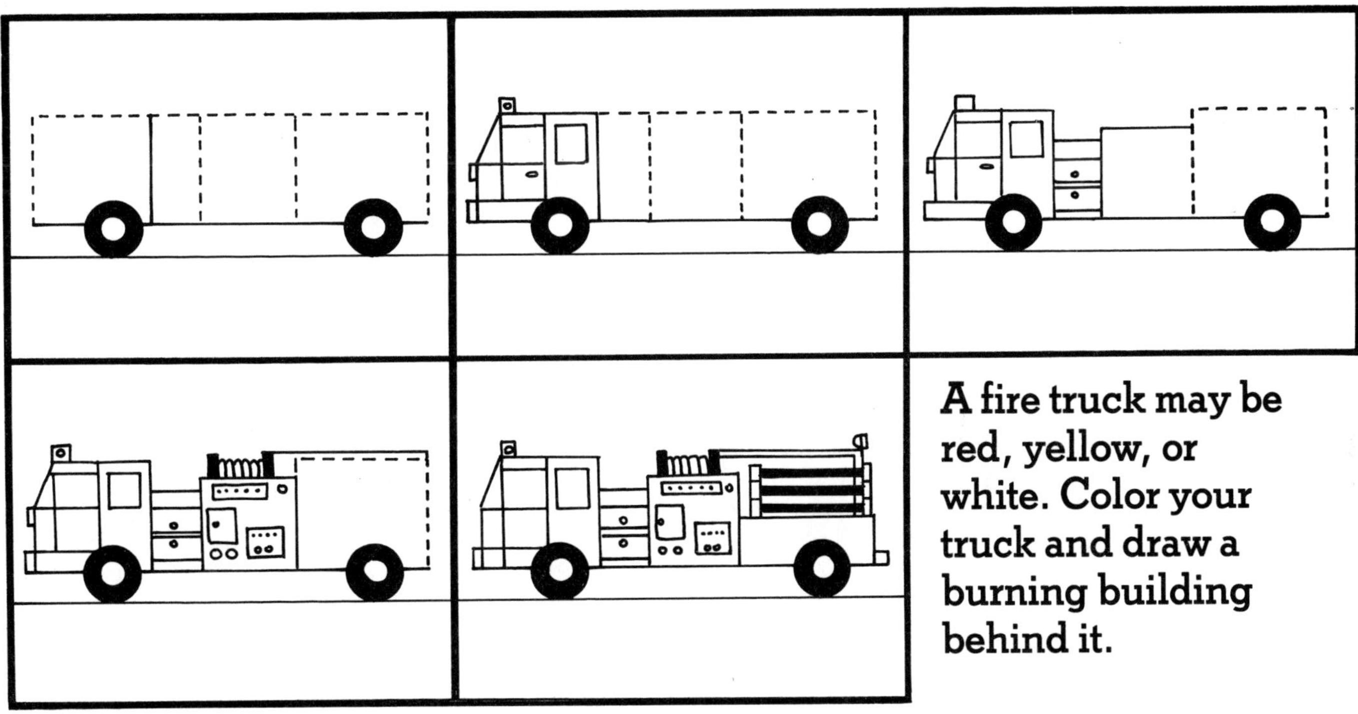

A fire truck may be red, yellow, or white. Color your truck and draw a burning building behind it.

forklift

Draw a forklift moving a huge crate, stack of lumber, boulder, or other large load.

Formula One racer

Draw several of these very fast cars that are speeding together in a close race.

galleon

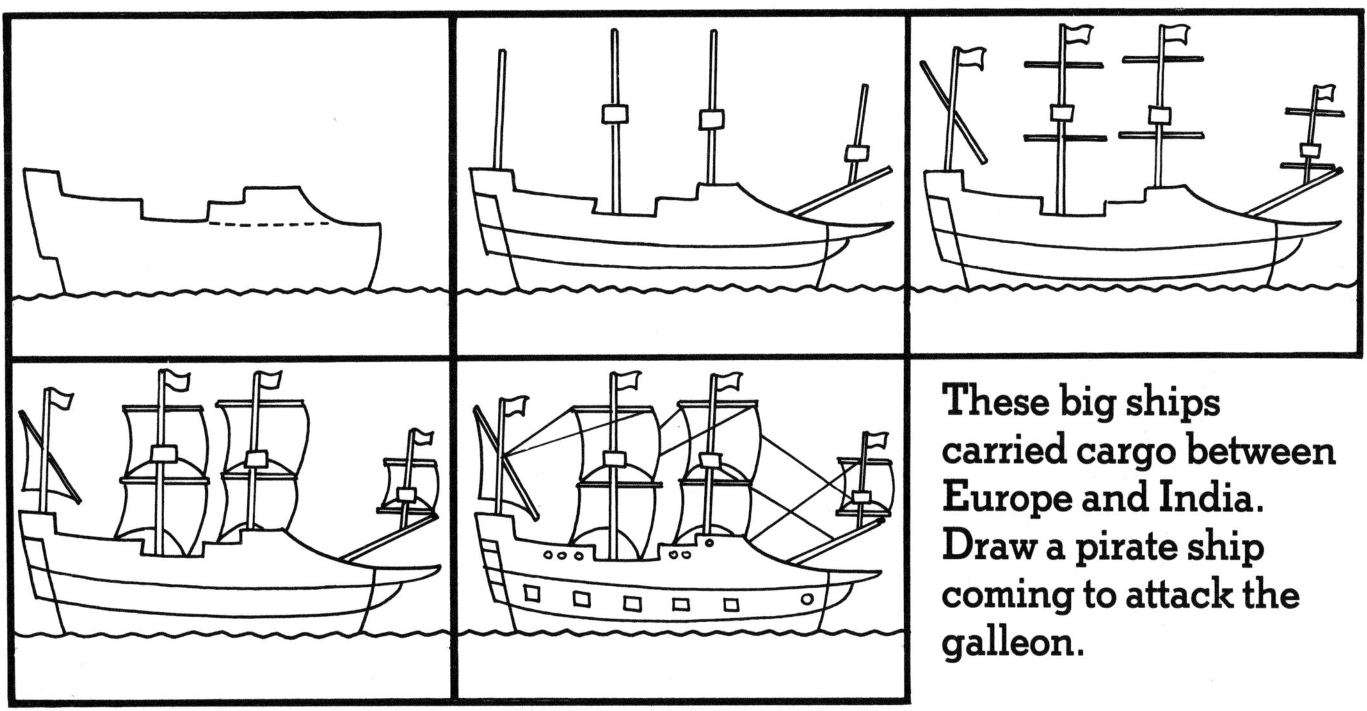

These big ships carried cargo between Europe and India. Draw a pirate ship coming to attack the galleon.

Huskie helicopter

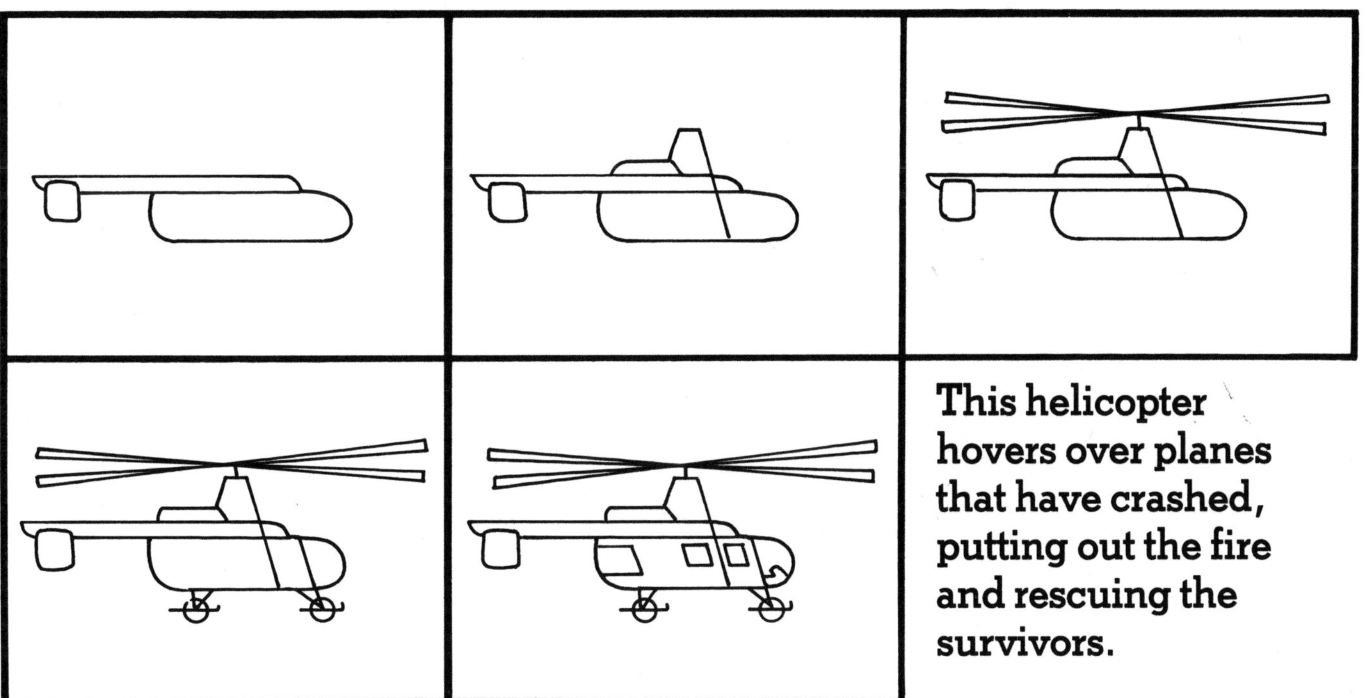

This helicopter hovers over planes that have crashed, putting out the fire and rescuing the survivors.

Indy car

Use tracing paper to draw several overlapping cars.

jet fighter

Draw a trio of these sleek planes silhouetted against a blazing sunset.

loader

Draw one of these powerful machines shoving rocks or dirt into an enormous pile.

locomotive

Draw a locomotive chugging past factories, snowy mountains, or a farm.

midget racer

Think of a name for this racer and write it on the side of the car. Add other designs and markings if you wish.

motor home

Draw a motor home that is rolling through a forest, along a beach, or past high mountains.

Reo runabout

Draw a dog sitting on the seat of your runabout, excited and ready for a ride.

river boat

Draw two river boats in a race with smoke pouring from their smokestacks.

Skyhook helicopter

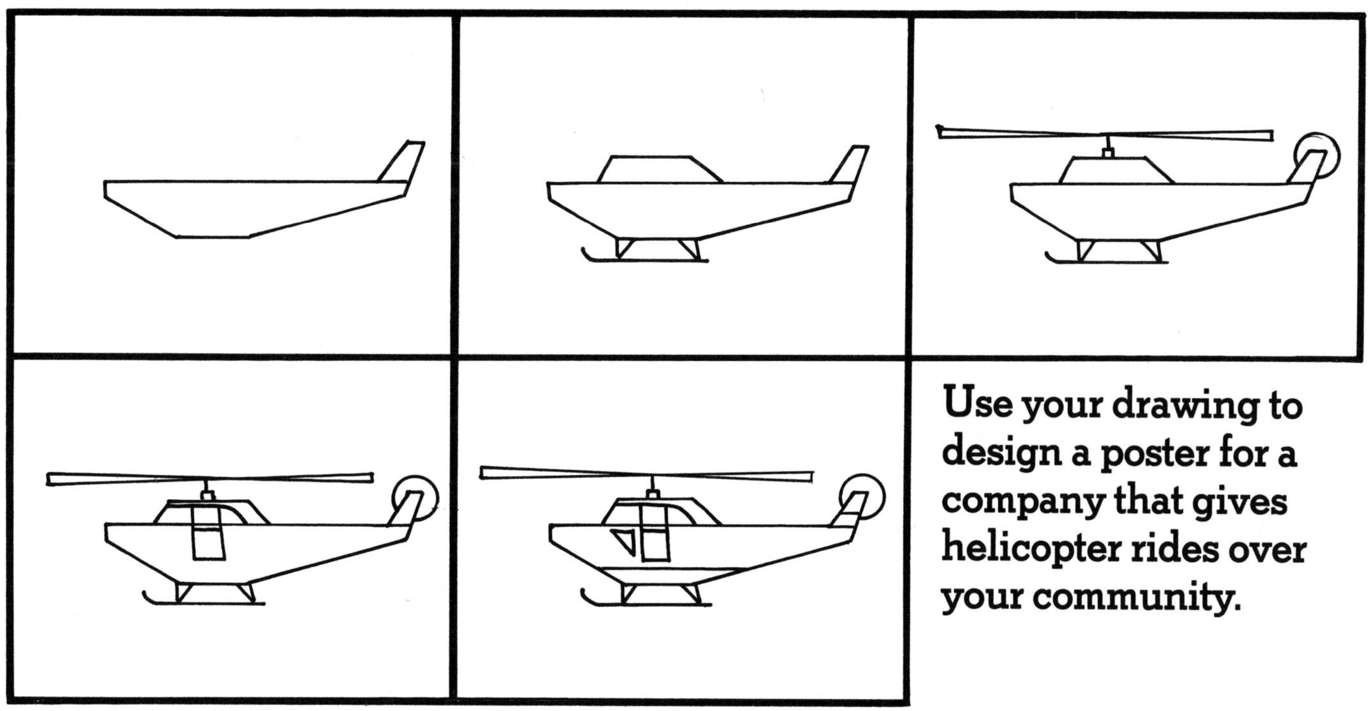

Use your drawing to design a poster for a company that gives helicopter rides over your community.

space shuttle

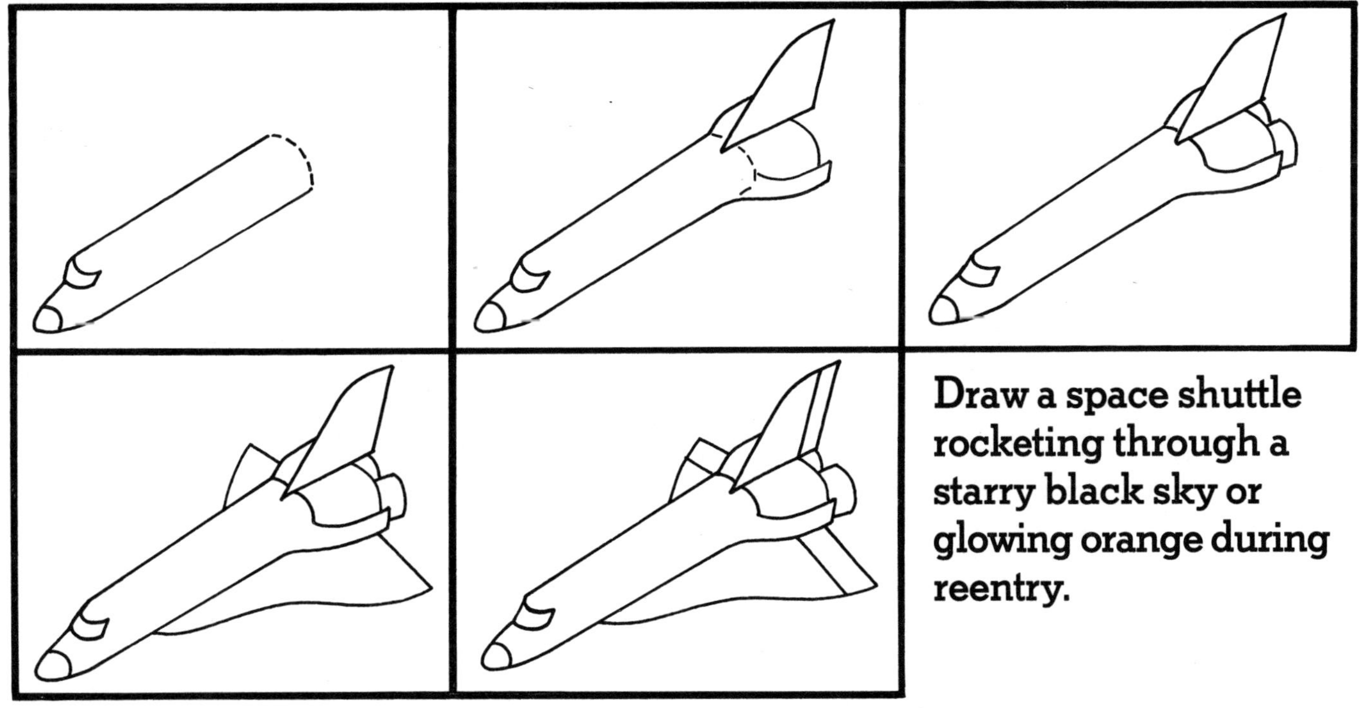

Draw a space shuttle rocketing through a starry black sky or glowing orange during reentry.

speedboat

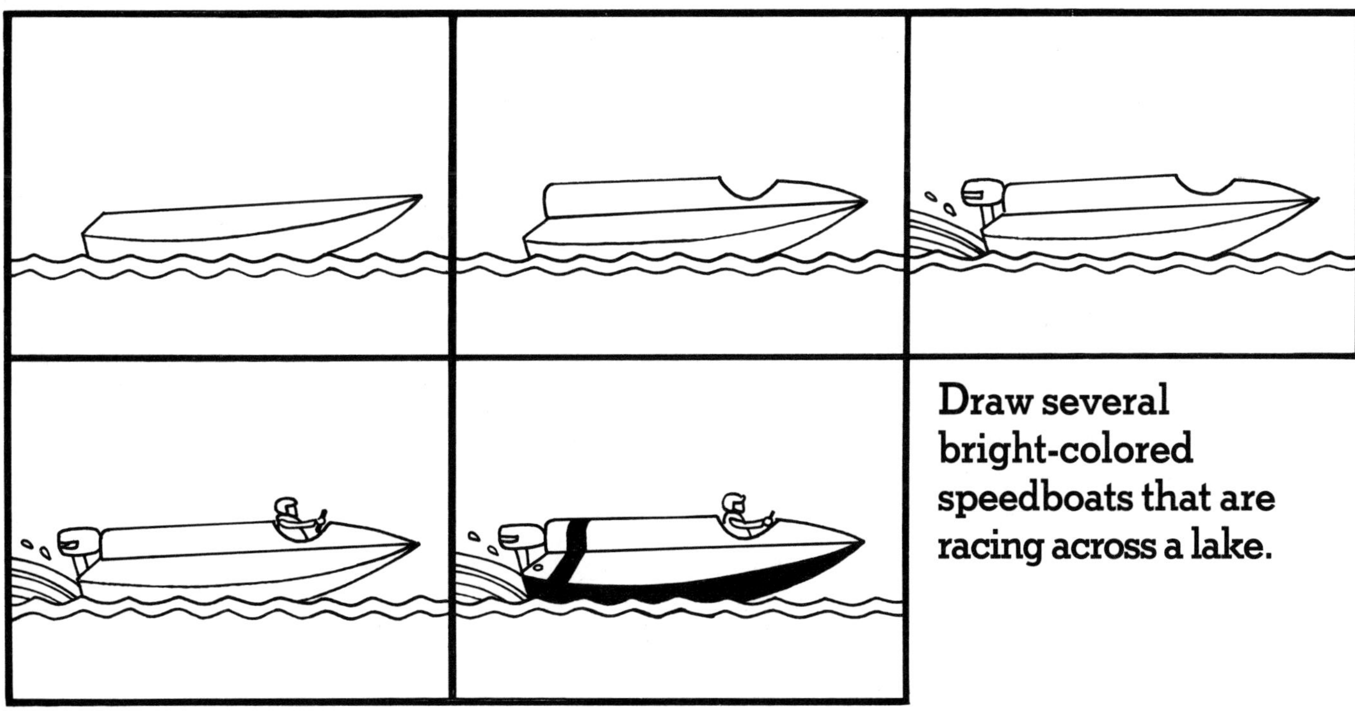

Draw several bright-colored speedboats that are racing across a lake.

street sweeper

Draw this street sweeper at work, picking up trash and leaving the street clean and neat.

submersible

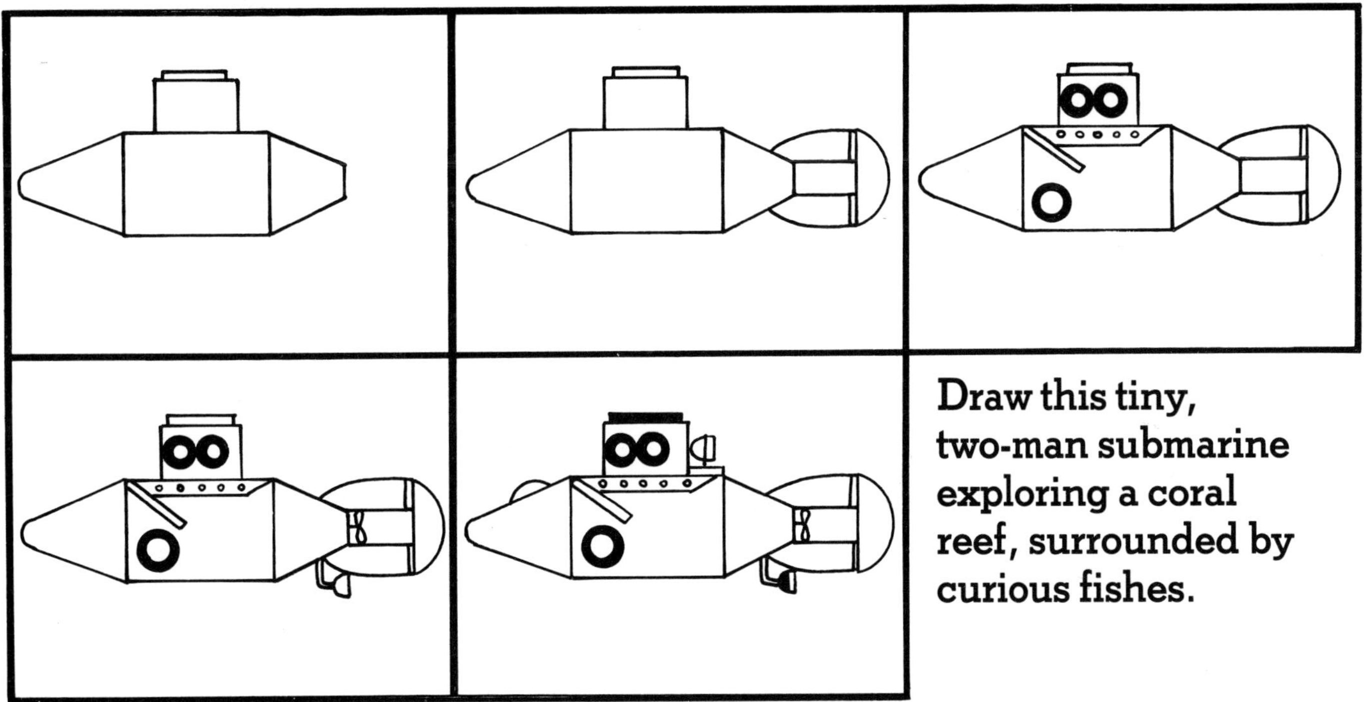

Draw this tiny, two-man submarine exploring a coral reef, surrounded by curious fishes.

tractor

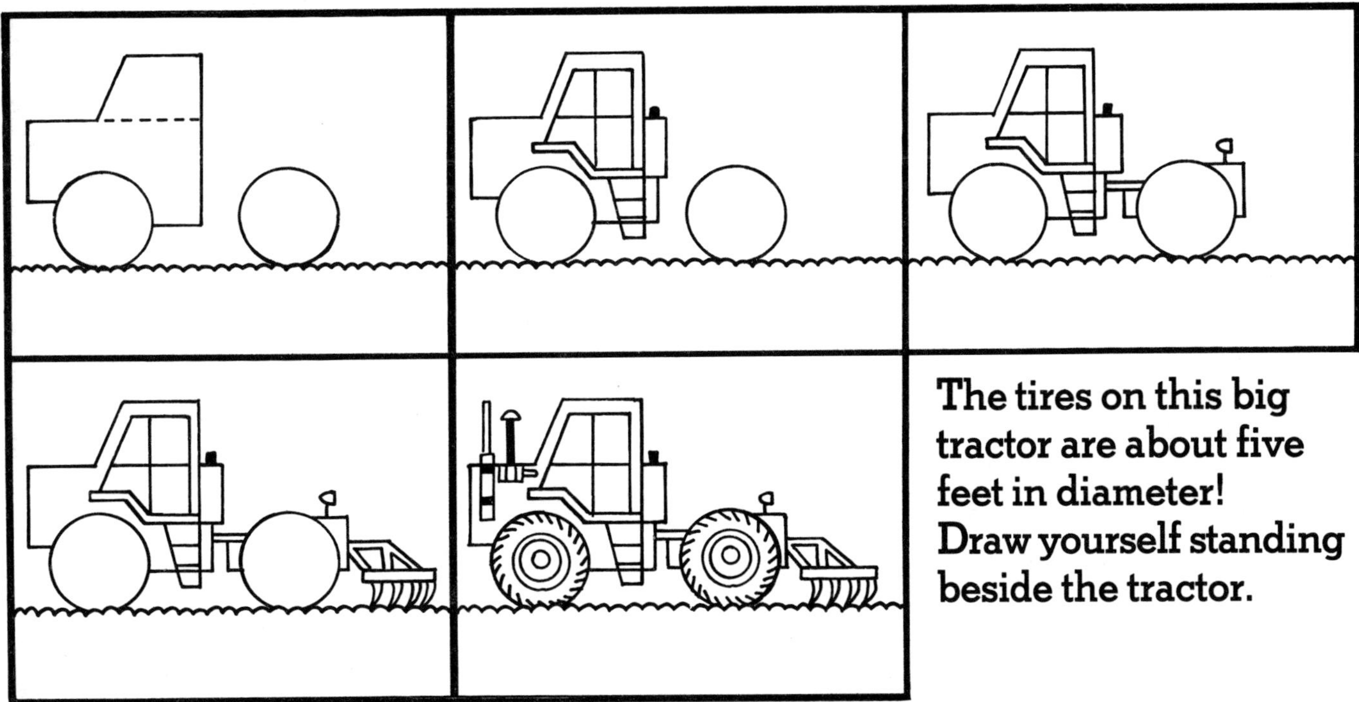

The tires on this big tractor are about five feet in diameter! Draw yourself standing beside the tractor.

trail bike

Draw someone riding this bike on a steep, bumpy mountain trail.

tugboat

Draw one of these powerful little boats pushing a big ship or pulling a string of barges.

Viking ship

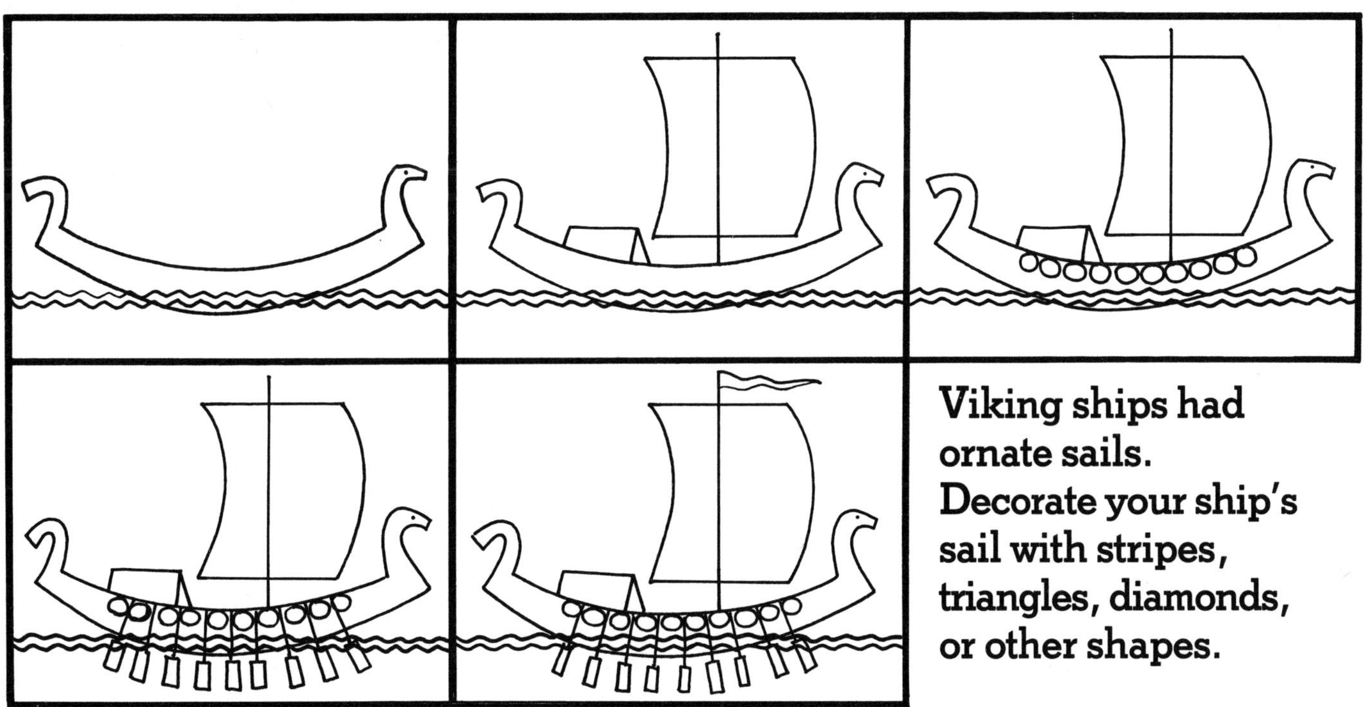

Viking ships had ornate sails. Decorate your ship's sail with stripes, triangles, diamonds, or other shapes.